USING MAKERSPACES FOR SCHOOL PROJECTS™

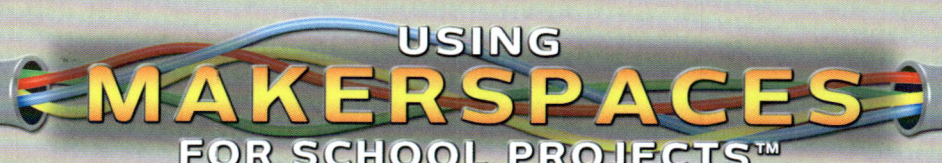

10 GREAT MAKERSPACE PROJECTS USING SOCIAL STUDIES

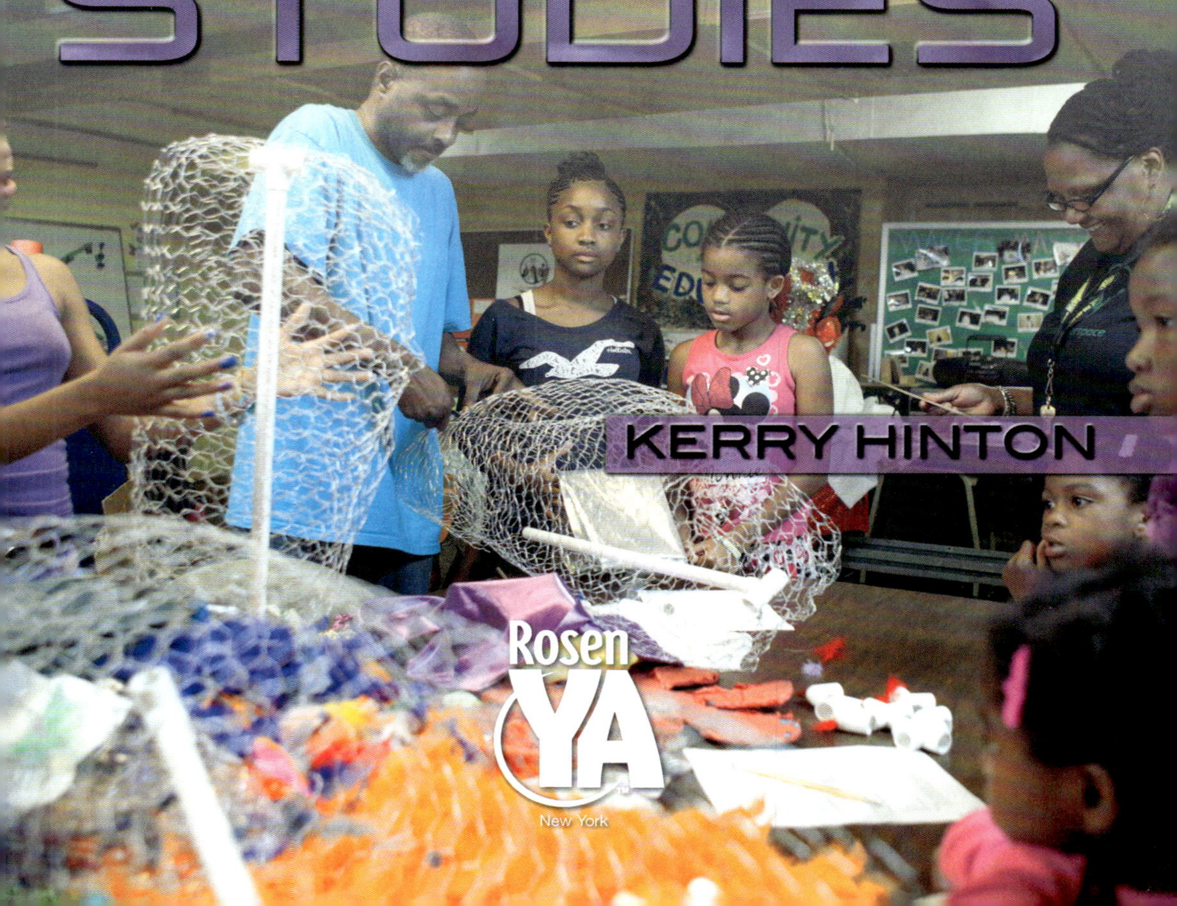

KERRY HINTON

Rosen YA
New York

Published in 2018 by The Rosen Publishing Group, Inc.
29 East 21st Street, New York, NY 10010

Copyright © 2018 by The Rosen Publishing Group, Inc.

First Edition

All rights reserved. No part of this book may be reproduced in any form without permission in writing from the publisher, except by a reviewer.

Library of Congress Cataloging-in-Publication Data

Names: Hinton, Kerry, author.
Title: 10 great makerspace projects using social studies / Kerry Hinton.
Other titles: Ten great makerspace projects using social studies
Description: First edition. | New York : Rosen Publishing, 2018. | Series: Using makerspaces for school projects | Includes bibliographical references and index. | Audience: Grade 6 to 12.
Identifiers: LCCN 2016055905 | ISBN 9781499438505 (library bound book)
Subjects: LCSH: Makerspaces—Juvenile literature. | Social sciences—Study and teaching—Activity programs—Juvenile literature.
Classification: LCC TS171.57 .H46 2017 | DDC 372.89—dc23
LC record available at https://lccn.loc.gov/2016055905

Manufactured in the United States of America

CONTENTS

INTRODUCTION 5

CHAPTER ONE
Social Studies: What Is It, Really? 7

CHAPTER TWO
Making: A History and Present Applications 14

CHAPTER THREE
Bringing It All Together 22

CHAPTER FOUR
Arts and Crafts Projects 29

CHAPTER FIVE
Laser and Vinyl Cutter Projects 37

CHAPTER SIX
Audio and Video Projects 43

CHAPTER SEVEN
3D-Printing Projects 50

GLOSSARY 57
FOR MORE INFORMATION 58
FOR FURTHER READING 60
BIBLIOGRAPHY 61
INDEX 62

INTROD

Today there are more than a thousand makerspaces and hackerspaces around the planet. This is more than ten times the number of these spaces there were ten years ago.

INTRODUCTION

Over the last thirty years, the tech advances mankind has made have been constant and frequent. Our televisions, computers, and video games have developed so much that it would seem unbelievable to people who lived just a century ago. Even the way we make things in the twenty-first century is different. In the past, manufacturing was limited to companies that had the large and expensive equipment to make the things we need and use every day. We are nearing a point where we will be able to do it from the comfort of our homes. Until that day comes, we have an alternative: makerspaces.

Makerspaces are centers of imagination and creativity where people of all ages can experiment with tools and technology. Until their existence, the average person would not have been able to walk into a manufacturing facility and use expensive computers and million-dollar machines. Access to many complex tools has become cheaper and much more available to the average citizen. The range of what can be made is impressive. People can sew, program, and fabricate almost anything from sock puppets to car parts. Makerspaces can be found in factories, libraries, schools, and even buses!

There are makerspaces on almost every continent on our planet. Some of them share projects and ideas with one another as they learn and create across man-made borders. Making is fun, but it also connects with what we learn in the classroom. It gives us the ability to improve our lives and bring the residents of our global village closer.

10 GREAT MAKERSPACE PROJECTS USING SOCIAL STUDIES

The projects in this book will help you better understand the connection between social studies and making. As you work through them, remember that every step of this process is a learning experience. There are no time limits and no rewards for getting it right the first time. The real reward is learning and then building on that to tackle other challenges.

CHAPTER ONE
Social Studies: What Is It, Really?

Most students take social studies at some point during school, but it may be hard to define. Is it history? Geography? Yes, yes—and quite a bit more. Actually, many other fields of studies are included under the umbrella that we call social studies.

Social studies is the study of the way people behave, connect, and work with one another all over the world. If this sounds broad, that's because it is. When you finish school, you will be a citizen of the world. Understanding that world is more important than ever. Technology is shortening the distance between people around the globe every day. Our neighbors don't just live next door to us anymore—your online neighborhood is getting bigger.

The National Council for the Social Studies tells us that social studies promotes "knowledge of and involvement in civic affairs ... such as health care, crime, and foreign policy." It's a big, wide world, and understanding it takes a big, wide base of knowledge. Social studies pulls knowledge from many subjects, including:

10 GREAT MAKERSPACE PROJECTS USING SOCIAL STUDIES

History. The study of the past.
Sociology. How humans and societies grow and develop.
Anthropology. The study of humans and their ancestors.
Political Science and Law. The study of government systems, politics, and the laws that govern them.
Economics. The study of the use and sale of goods and services.
Geography. The study of Earth's surface, cities, climate, and natural features such as bodies of water, mountains, and deserts.

Since it covers so many different subjects, social studies enables us to take a wide view of how we are all connected.

SOCIAL STUDIES: WHAT IS IT, REALLY?

In the world of the social sciences, all of these disciplines are connected. As technology grows, so does our ability to connect with people around the world. People connect in many different ways, not only from day to day but also from country to country. Not everyone enjoys the same living conditions. There are so many different things that affect this, including geography, climate, economics, and population. We study all the different subjects that make up social studies to understand not only our world but the world as other people have experienced it, in the past and also today.

Aside from the world at large, social studies is also concerned with the world that's closer to us. In order to be good global citizens, we need to be good citizens at home. This is called civics—it's the study of our government and how we relate to it as citizens.

SOCIAL STUDIES, MEET SOCIAL MEDIA

Social media websites and apps such as Facebook, Twitter, and Skype are among the most popular on the planet. They connect people through nearly instant communication. But social media has many uses besides entertainment. It has helped make the world smaller for everyone, including global makers of all skill levels. Sometimes, news can break on social media before it's even reported by newspapers or digital news sources.

10 GREAT MAKERSPACE PROJECTS USING SOCIAL STUDIES

Benjamin Franklin: One of Our First Makers

Ben Franklin's interests ranged from science and inventing to writing. During his lifetime, he also owned a printing press and served as ambassador to France.

You may know Ben Franklin (1706–1790) as one of the writers of the Declaration of Independence and the Constitution. If these were his only accomplishments, Franklin would be remembered for all time. Surprisingly, they weren't! When he wasn't busy helping create modern democracy, Ben Franklin also wrote books, started a volunteer fire department, and ran a printing business.

And then there's Ben Franklin the inventor. In 1742, he

SOCIAL STUDIES: WHAT IS IT, REALLY?

invented the Franklin Stove, which used less fuel to make more heat and less smoke. Since stoves were the main method of indoor heat in winter, this was a welcome invention.

Franklin also invented bifocal glasses, the first rocking chair, and swimming fins! He even created the armonica (also sometimes called the glass harmonica). Ludwig van Beethoven and Wolfgang Amadeus Mozart, two of the most famous classical composers of the modern world, used this instrument.

Ben Franklin was a self-taught maker whose curiosity crossed the boundaries of specific subjects. This led him to experiment with electricity, mapmaking, and medical science. This spirit can still be felt in makerspaces today.

There's even a social media network especially for the making community called MakerSpace. It is a great way for hopeful and experienced makers to connect and share ideas. Its design is similar to other popular social media sites, including a news feed.

When we post on social media, we're updating friends and family on what is happening *right now*. Social studies connects this to the past. It's a helpful tool to see how the past influences the present and the future.

10 GREAT MAKERSPACE PROJECTS USING SOCIAL STUDIES

SOCIAL STUDIES AND MAKING

People have always been creating and inventing. Making dates back thousands of years. Our great inventors were makers—Thomas Edison and others tinkered and experimented

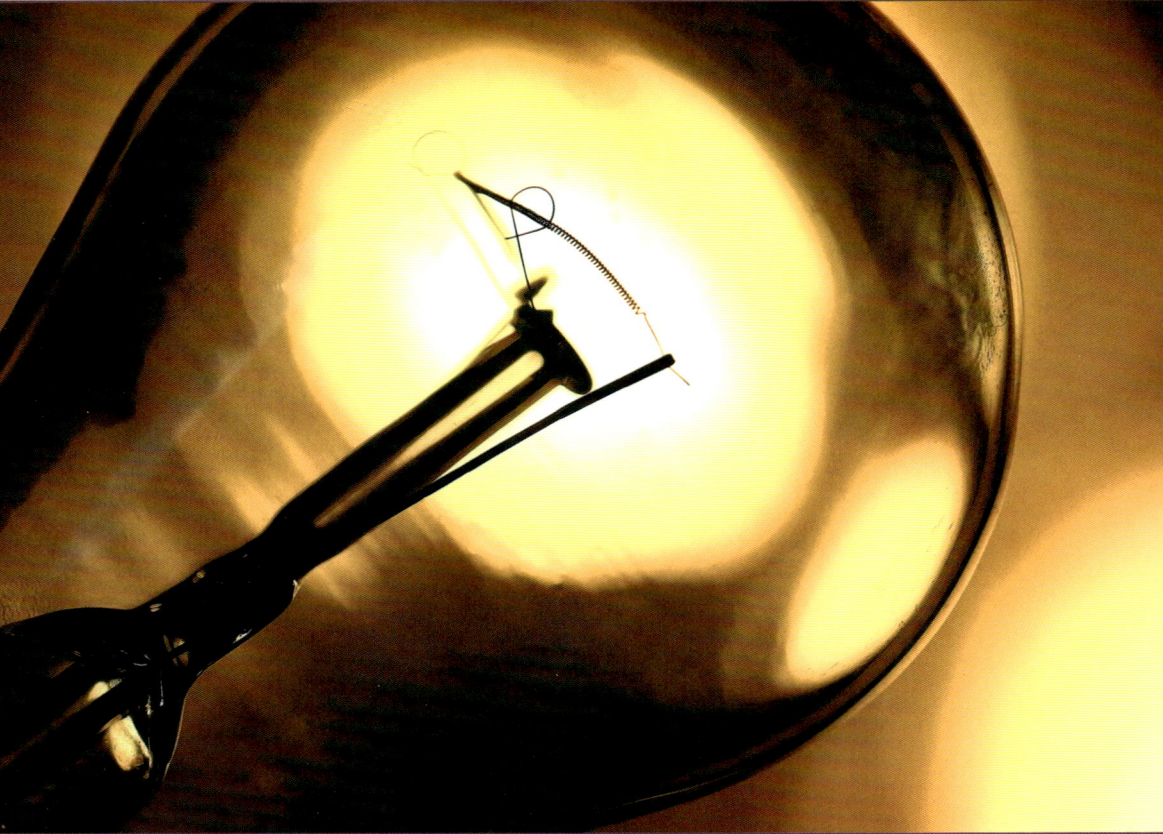

Makers and other creative people have been solving problems and creating new devices throughout history. They will undoubtedly do the same in the future.

SOCIAL STUDIES: WHAT IS IT, REALLY?

with electricity. The result? Lights around the world, which improved lives. Makers helped build the United States and Canada—if a person had to solve a problem where no solution existed, he or she was embracing his or her inner maker.

What makes today's makerspaces different from hobby shops, workshops, and creative spaces of the past is the concept of community. It's the heart of the maker movement. Sharing, making mistakes, fine tuning, and remixing are what makes making fun! Makerspaces are also collaborative and democratic. Most projects don't have "bosses" or people in charge. Adults and other makers are always happy to give help and direction, though.

Making and social studies share a goal: to expand the global community and to understand people in order to make life for everyone as good as it can be. We use makerspaces to build for enjoyment and learning, but we're also creating understanding and change.

Now that we have some background, let's take a closer look at the ideas and tools of the learning laboratories we call makerspaces.

CHAPTER TWO
MAKING: A HISTORY AND PRESENT APPLICATIONS

You may have noticed that other names besides "makerspace" are used for similar facilities. No matter what the name may be (Fab Labs, hackerspaces, and TechShops), they have one goal: creative making.

Fab Labs are fabrication laboratories. They're a network of makerspaces around the world that share information and use the same equipment to fabricate things. Hackerspaces were originally dedicated to programming and coding. Today, hacking means so much more than the original computer hackers could have imagined. There are websites with instructions on how to "hack" furniture, electronics, and even your life.

Some makerspaces do not get funding and rely on membership fees or crowdfunding to keep their spaces open. You may have to pay for access at some of them. Some may be stand-alone and not set up for lab-to-lab sharing, but they still have plenty of makers and mentors to ask for advice and to share with.

MAKING: A HISTORY AND PRESENT APPLICATIONS

THE MAKING REVOLUTION BEGINS

The first modern makerspaces were born at the Massachusetts Institute of Technology (MIT) in 1998. Professor Neil Gershenfeld taught a class called How to Make (Almost) Anything. The course investigated the overlap between

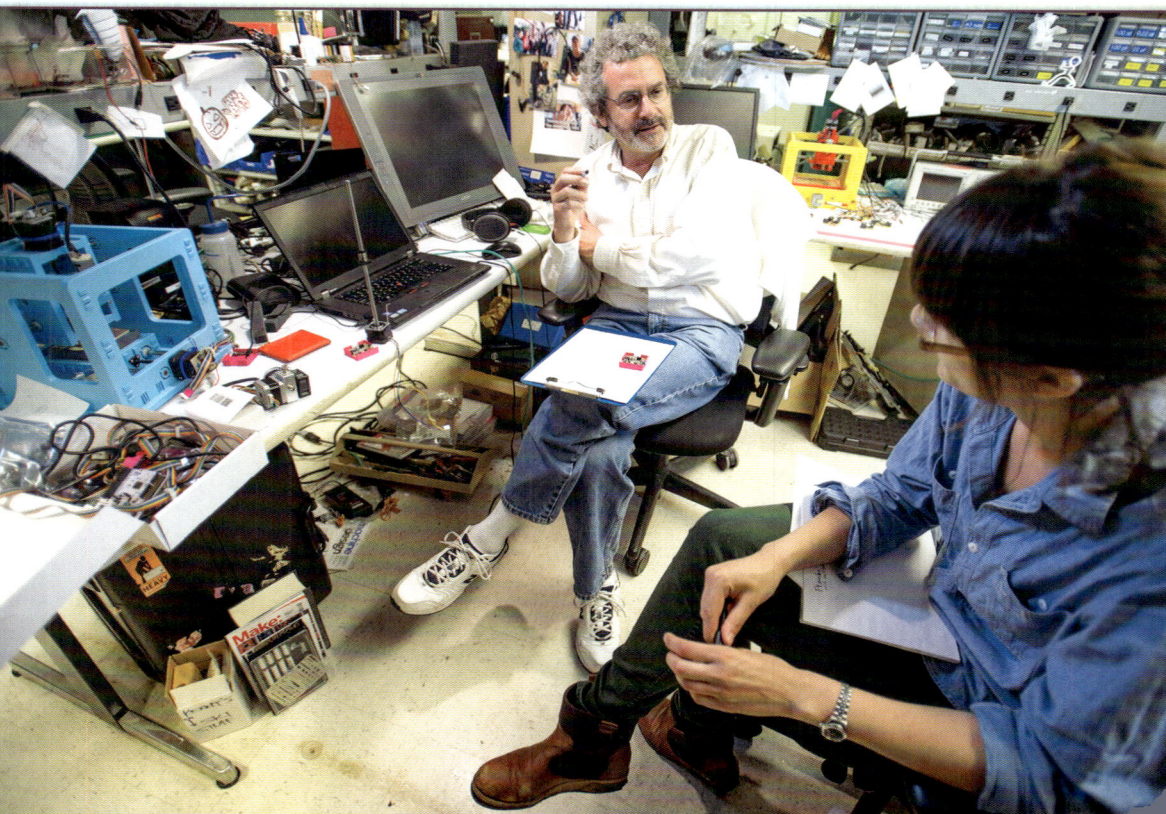

Neil Gershenfeld and the Fab Lab movement were instrumental in the spread of maker culture around the globe.

10 GREAT MAKERSPACE PROJECTS USING SOCIAL STUDIES

computer science and physical science. The class had access to a large facility filled with industrial equipment that could "make and measure things that are as small as atoms or as large as buildings."

Many of the students in that first class did not have many computer or technology skills. As the class went on, they realized that these machines could help them in their own fields. What started out as a class became a creative workshop. Both creative and scientific students saw the potential of digital fabrication. This was the birth of the Fab Lab.

TODAY'S MAKERSPACES

Things began to happen quickly after the first Fab Lab opened in 2005. That same year saw the launch of *Make:* magazine. Making became even more popular with the first Maker Faire, which was held the next year in San Mateo, California. In 2010, Maker Faires were also held in Detroit, Michigan, and New York City. They're a great way for people to socialize and collaborate in the ever-growing maker movement.

Technology is an important feature of makerspaces, but when keeping social studies in mind, we should always keep one foot in the past. What we now consider common knowledge was the peak of technology for past cultures and societies. Today, the average citizen can build or design almost anything he or she can imagine. When we create and share across different disciplines, we can get a better understanding of our world.

THE MAKERSPACE TOOLBOX

Now that we know what makerspaces are, let's discuss what tools are available in them. The size and budget of a particular space will have a direct effect on what kind and how many of certain tools you may find within. We'll explore some of them in more depth as they relate to our projects.

With the exception of Fab Labs (because member labs sign a charter agreement on what equipment must be included in facilities), not every makerspace has the same equipment. Some of the tools and materials you can use are listed below. If you're curious about any of these tools and what they can do, take a trip to the nearest makerspace and see them in action.

Traditional Tools. These are the non-computer-controlled tools you can use to build or create. They include hammers, sewing machines, power tools, and tools for welding and working with wood and metal.

Computers. Screens and keyboards are essential to makerspaces. They can take our ideas, translate them into digital instructions, and send them to a variety of machines and devices to make them real. They're used in 3D printing, making music, video, and animation.

3D Scanners. A 3D scanner can take a digital three-dimensional picture of a real object and convert it to a computer image or model. This is known as 3D modeling. Once a scan is complete, the data can be saved. Using computer-aided design (CAD) software, these

10 GREAT MAKERSPACE PROJECTS USING SOCIAL STUDIES

models can be examined and adjusted before they are sent to a 3D printer.

3D Printers. 3D printers receive their instructions from a 3D-modeling program that allows a 3D design to be broken down into parts and printed layer by layer. Instead of ink, many 3D printers use spools of filament made of plastic or another material that is heated and used to

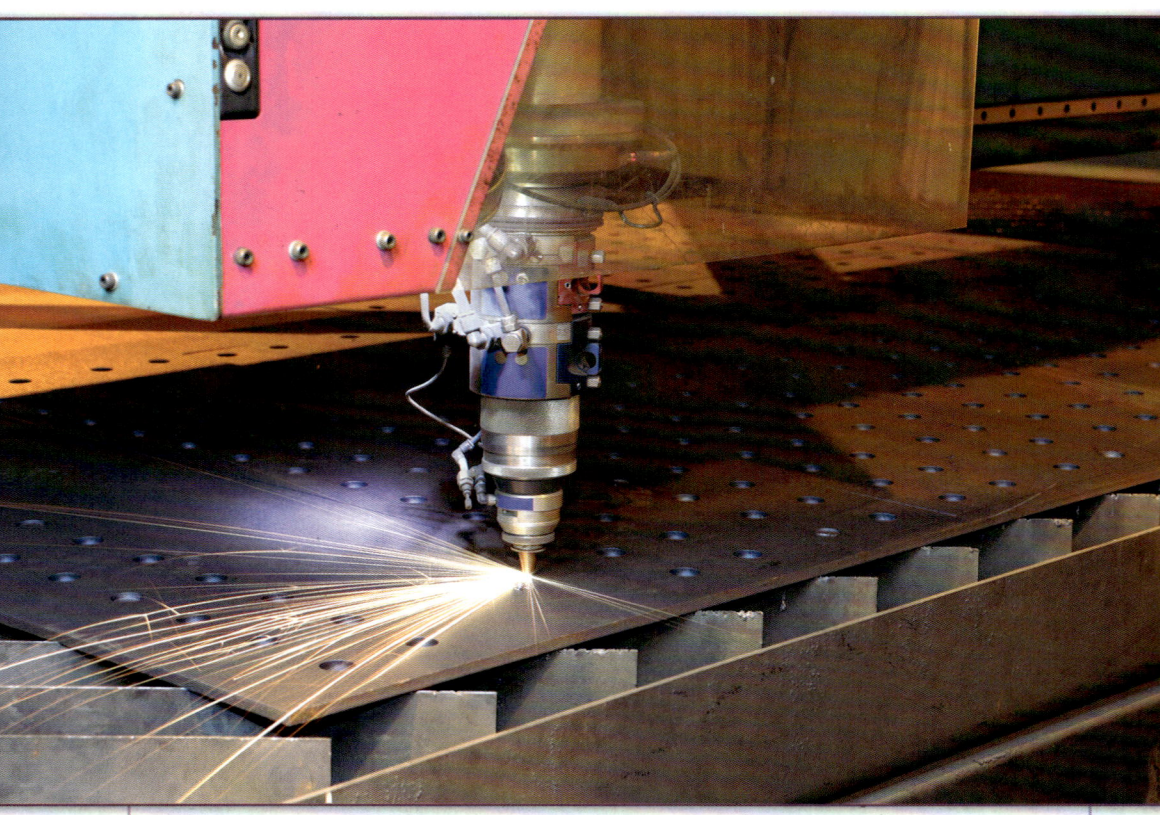

Laser cutters can be used to cut anything from clothing to metal to food.

MAKING: A HISTORY AND PRESENT APPLICATIONS

build something layer by layer. Most 3D printers found in makerspaces are desktop printers, so the size of what users can make is often limited.

Laser Cutters and Vinyl Cutters. These tools are used to make precise cuts in thin metals, plastics, and foam. Laser cutters use a powerful focused light to make cuts, while vinyl cutters use a sharp blade. They get their instructions from digital files.

You'll also find a variety of other materials in makerspaces. These include:

Office Supplies. These are made up of paper clips, rubber bands, notebooks, and especially paper—it's good for sketching, making early models, and on its own for projects.

CAUTION! MAKERSPACE SAFETY

Making things is fun, but getting hurt isn't. The machines that have the potential to build amazing things also have the potential to seriously injure you. When working on these projects, an experienced adult should always be present. Before you work with any piece of equipment in a space, be sure to learn about it and find out what the precautions are for using it.

Laser cutters, drills, and blades are all dangerous, and you'll need to be familiar with

(continued on the next page)

10 GREAT MAKERSPACE PROJECTS USING SOCIAL STUDIES

(continued from the previous page)

the safety rules for each piece of equipment. Safety glasses are always a must. Also, be sure you have a first-aid kit nearby in case you need to treat a burn, a cut, or eye damage. Fire is another potential danger. Know where the fire extinguishers are in your space and how to use them. Spaces should always be ventilated. Fumes from chemicals and small particles from cutting and grinding can affect breathing. Also be sure to work efficiently. Organization and planning will not only make your project better but also safer.

Recycled Stuff. Things an ordinary person may get rid of can be gold to makers. Cardboard, used bottles and cans, and plastics can all be reclaimed to form the base of many projects.

Used Things. Many makerspaces take contributions and donations that would otherwise be headed for the landfill. This includes old electronics, phones, furniture, carpeting, and much more.

Scraps. Sometimes, scraps and leftovers from current projects can be used again on later ones. Makers like to throw away as little as possible.

Nature. Don't forget about the world around you—the sun, wind, and rain are all great things to use or study for projects. Dirt, trees, and leaves are other natural resources that can also spark your imagination.

MAKING: A HISTORY AND PRESENT APPLICATIONS

Arduino. Arduino is an open-source platform that uses programmable circuit boards to connect to computers to perform tasks.

Raspberry Pi. This little credit-card-sized computer is much more powerful than it looks. It's relatively easy to program and use, even for newbies with limited computer experience.

Robotics and Construction Sets. There are dozens of companies that make kits for robotics, including Play-i (now Wonder Workshop) and Lego. No matter the brand, these kits and sets let kids of all ages build some really cool robots.

CHAPTER THREE
Bringing It All Together

Making involves problem solving using many school subjects. A strong background in science is going to be important in coming years. The more preparation and knowledge both current and future makers have, the better. This idea can be summed up by one acronym: STEAM.

STEAM: SCIENCE, TECHNOLOGY, ENGINEERING, ART, AND MATH

STEAM is an acronym that stands for science, technology, engineering, art, and math. It connects science and math with the creativity and innovation of art and other subjects. Much of what you study in school will involve it in the future:

Art. Art students can scan and manipulate models, sculptures, or other pieces.

History. Digital archives of historical documents, ancient civilizations, or geography can make the past much more real and accessible to people who may not be able to travel to see the real artifacts.

Math. 3D scanning and computer-aided design (CAD) programs can help us examine geometrical shapes and explain difficult concepts.

BRINGING IT ALL TOGETHER

Libraries—Not Just for Books Anymore

Before you could access a world of information on a personal computer or smartphone, the local library was the primary information center for communities around Canada and the United States. In the words of author Phillip Torrone,

Public libraries have become centers of creativity and computing for twenty-first-century makers. They have taken the makerspace into the community.

(continued on the next page)

10 GREAT MAKERSPACE PROJECTS USING SOCIAL STUDIES

(continued from the previous page)

"They symbolize what is most important, a commitment to educating the next generation."

The first library to start a makerspace was the Fayetteville Free Library in Fayetteville, New York. A graduate student named Lauren Smedey wrote a paper outlining her ideas for a great collaboration: libraries and makerspaces. In it, she said, "Public libraries exist to provide free and open access to information, technology and ideas. Building a makerspace (what we're calling a Fabulous Laboratory) at the FFL will provide our community with the opportunity to have free access to this world-changing technology."

The FFL Fabulous Laboratory opened in 2011. It's free to use and accepts private funding and donations. Today, libraries in schools and communities around North America are filled with creative students eager to learn more, make more, and waste less.

Design. The planning and design of a project is a great time for learning. Using computers to do this lets us make mistakes, learn from them, and correct them on our way to solutions.

Biology. Students can look at 3D scans of plants, animals, or organs to understand them in greater depth.

BRINGING IT ALL TOGETHER

Law. In a world where we can make (almost) anything, legal issues are bound to pop up, especially in terms of copyright and ownership. Lawyers must understand the technology in order to understand the laws for it.

As you can see, making and makerspaces have the potential to change almost every aspect of daily life on our planet. This is why social studies and maker culture are so important to one another.

Now, let's get started on our very first project.

PROJECT 1: MAKE ANCIENT EGYPTIAN PAPYRUS

Although we use digital tools more and more, we still rely on paper. We use it every day for writing, packaging, and many other things. Paper as we know it was invented in ancient China by Cai Lun (202 BCE–220 BCE). Before paper was invented, there was papyrus (PUH-pie-RUSS). It was made from the pith of the Cyperus papyrus plant. Pith is a spongy material found in the stem of the plant. Ancient Egyptians weren't the only ancient people to make primitive paper from this plant. Greek and Roman peoples also used papyrus for writing. Papyrus is thicker and stiffer than modern paper. Although the word "paper" comes from "papyrus," the two are not the same. Making paper today is a complex industrialized process compared to the small batches people made thousands of years ago. Don't have access to a papyrus plant? Don't worry—you can still make your own!

SKILL LEVEL

Easy

In their time, ancient Egyptians joined sheets of papyrus to make long scrolls that functioned as books.

BRINGING IT ALL TOGETHER

TIME

1 hour

BASIC MATERIALS

Newspaper or a drop cloth	Paintbrush
Instant coffee (3–4 tablespoons)	Drawing paper (or 3–4 paper bags)
Water (1 cup)	Felt-tipped pen or marker

OPTIONAL MATERIALS

Matches
Candle

STEPS

1. Lay down some newspaper or a drop cloth to protect your work surface.
2. Add a small amount of instant coffee to your water and stir.
3. Dip your paintbrush in the water.
4. Paint your paper with the coffee and water mixture. Add more coffee to make the mixture darker if you choose.
5. Let the paper dry. Repaint if necessary.
6. Turn the paper over and paint the other side.
7. Once it's dry, you're finished! Write whatever you'd like on your "papyrus."

OPTIONAL STEPS (ONLY WITH ADULT SUPERVISION)

1. Light a match and use it to *gently* burn the edges of your paper to make it look even more aged.
2. Light a candle. After it burns for a few minutes, let some wax drip on your paper to make a wax seal. The type of pen and brush you choose is up to you.

There are many different kinds of markers—experiment on plain paper before you make your papyrus for the best look. Paintbrushes vary in size, too. The only rule here is to pick one that can fit in your water cup.

CHAPTER FOUR
Arts and Crafts Projects

Although so much creative work can be done with computers and advanced equipment, it's important to remember that there are plenty of things you can do in a makerspace with tools that don't rely on computer controls. The projects in this chapter use some making skills that have been in use since long before the computer age began. Remember, social studies isn't only about what's happening now; it's also about connecting the past to the present. Combining old and new technologies is part of connecting to our shared history. Now let's create!

PROJECT 2: MAKE A SEAWORTHY PADDLEBOAT

Before the invention of the airplane, boats provided the only way to cross the ocean. Mankind has been traveling by boat for thousands of years. Some of the first boats were primitive canoes made in ancient Egypt. Back then, paddles didn't even exist yet—people used their hands to move through the water. As time went on, improvements were made. Oars and rudders made boats easier to steer and move. The biggest advancement was the use of wind to fill sails made of cloth. By the fifteenth century, more sails were added, making ships faster than ever. These new speedy ships helped settlers explore and settle the New World.

As time went on, iron replaced wood, and engines were added, making boats safer and faster. Today's modern engines allow ships to cross oceans in days instead of weeks. The world wouldn't be the same without them. The ability to float is called buoyancy. Objects can float on water if they weigh less than the amount of water they displace, or move. If your project is a success, you can always increase the materials and dimensions and make a life-sized boat that can carry people!

SKILL LEVEL

Easy

TIME

1 hour

BASIC MATERIALS

4 wooden dowels (12" x 1" thick)	Rubber band
2 one-liter bottles	Tools
Glue gun	Ruler
Duct tape	Hacksaw
16 Popsicle sticks	

STEPS

1. Decide how wide you'd like the boat to be. Cut each dowel to that length.
2. Measure that distance between the bottles. The bottles should be lined up evenly.

ARTS AND CRAFTS PROJECTS

3. Attach the dowels to the bottles using a glue gun or duct tape. The front dowel should be near the tops of the bottles just past the narrow part. The back dowel should be about three to four inches from the bottom of the bottles.

4. Attach one of each remaining dowel to the outer side of each bottle. The dowels should be attached halfway between the top of the boat and its bottom. These dowels will hold your rubber band and paddle. Reinforce them with duct tape.

5. Make your paddle. Lay eight sticks side by side and glue them together (or use duct tape). Place the remaining eight sticks on top and glue or tape them to the other sticks. Make sure the paddle will reach the water from the side dowels.

6. Make sure your rubber band is long enough to stretch between the side dowels. Place the paddle directly in the middle of the rubber band. Glue the paddle to the rubber band and let it dry.

7. Twist the rubber band and paddle until it is tight.

8. Place the boat in the water and release the rubber band. Your boat should glide through the water.

9. Tweak your creation by adding sails or more bottles to make the boat bigger.

PROJECT 3: MAKE A CIGAR BOX GUITAR

As long as there has been music, people have been interested in making their own instruments. In areas where money was

10 GREAT MAKERSPACE PROJECTS USING SOCIAL STUDIES

Cigar box guitars and other homemade stringed instruments are called **chordophones**. The vibration of the strings sends sound vibrations through the air.

hard to come by, buying a guitar or piano was only a dream to many people. Enter the cigar box guitar. The first cigar box guitars appeared in the 1840s, around the same time that cigar makers began to ship their products in small, individual boxes instead of large crates. Before the birth of the phonograph and radio, playing an instrument was the only way many people in rural areas could bring music into their lives. Many country and blues artists from rural backgrounds were trained in this tradition.

In addition to guitars, cigar boxes were used to provide bodies for other stringed instruments including banjos, ukuleles, and violins. Not every stringed instrument made this way was primitive. At the National Cigar Box Museum in York, Pennsylvania, a few are on exhibit that are works of art. Today's hobbyists make, trade, and sell cigar box guitars, keeping this musical tradition alive for future generations.

ARTS AND CRAFTS PROJECTS

SKILL LEVEL

Medium to difficult

TIME

3–5 hours

BASIC MATERIALS

Cigar box (ask your local cigar or tobacco shop or order on eBay)	Bamboo skewer or wooden dowel (6" long and about ⅓" in diameter)
Wood (3 feet long and 1" x 2" wide)	Wood glue
Wood screws (6 sized ¼")	Guitar tuning pegs (2 or 3)
	Guitar strings (3)

TOOLS

Pencil
Ruler
Safety goggles
Hacksaw or coping saw

Sandpaper
¼", ¹⁄₁₆", and ½" drill bits
Wire cutters
Round file (optional)

NOTES

1. If you can, obtain a guitar before you begin. Experiment with it. It may make this project a little easier.

2. Try to get a cigar box made of heavy wood. It will sound better. Guitars use vibrating strings placed above a hollow or solid body to make sounds. These instruments are also called chordophones, which also includes violins and harps. When the strings vibrate, they cause the body of the guitar to resonate, sending the sound outward.
3. If you can't find a cigar box, you can substitute other materials to make the body of your guitar a piece of wood that's the same size.
4. If you don't have tuning pegs, you can use bolts and wing nuts as a substitute. You'll need three of each.
5. Make sure you choose a hard wood for your guitar neck. This will prevent the neck from bending, which can affect the sound. Oak and poplar are good choices.
6. You don't need guitar strings to make your guitar, although they will probably make your instrument sound better. You can also use nylon fishing line or string. As long as your guitar makes some noise, you have succeeded!

STEPS

Tuning pegs are used to keep stringed instruments in tune. They can be tightened or loosened to make the pitch higher or lower.

1. Use your pencil and ruler to measure an area ¼" deep and 5" long. Cut that area away using

ARTS AND CRAFTS PROJECTS

your hacksaw. This is going to be the neck of the guitar. The notch you cut will be the top of the guitar. If you need to, use sandpaper to smooth out your cut.

2. Measure ⅜" in from each side of the notch you just made. Use the ¼" drill bit to drill three holes (two on one side and one on the other) for your tuning pegs. Make sure the holes for the side with two tuning pegs are 1 ½" apart. The pegs should also be on the underside of the neck.
3. Measure ¾" up from the bottom of the notch you cut in step 1. Make three shallow, evenly spaced holes with the ¹⁄₁₆" drill bit. This will prevent the wood from splitting or getting damaged in the next step.
4. Use three screws in the holes. These screws will keep the guitar strings in the best position for sounding good.
5. Measure ¼" down from the bottom of your notch. Use a saw or a file to make a shallow groove at that spot.
6. Cut the wooden dowel to the same width as the neck. Use the wood glue and place the dowel in the groove you cut in step 5. This is called the nut on a guitar—it keeps the strings at the same height. Make three shallow grooves in the dowel for each string.
7. Measure 25 ½" down from the nut you made in step 6 and draw a pencil line. This line will be where you place another dowel. This will be your bridge. The bridge keeps the strings elevated above the body of the guitar like the nut does at the top of the neck.
8. Use a saw or a file to make a shallow groove at the bridge line.
9. Using the ¹⁄₁₆" bit, drill three holes at the bottom of the neck.

10 GREAT MAKERSPACE PROJECTS USING SOCIAL STUDIES

When you're finished, the guitar strings will be threaded through them and up to the tuning pegs. Each string has a piece of metal at the bottom to keep it in place.

10. Make sure the neck is smooth. Sand it again if you need to—this will prevent splinters.
11. Use the ½" drill bit to drill a hole in either corner of the cigar box (the hinged side). This sound hole will project the notes you play over a greater distance.
12. Measure the exact middle of the cigar box and mark it.
13. Measure 3" up from the bottom of the cigar box and mark it. When you attach the neck to the top of the cigar box, this mark should line up with the bridge.
14. Cut the wooden dowel to the same width as your neck. Use the wood glue and place the dowel in the bridge groove.
15. Open the cigar box and attach the neck to it from the inside of the box using the three remaining screws. The opening should be facing the bottom of the guitar.
16. From top to bottom, use the G, B, and D strings to string your guitar. Use an online reference for instructions.
17. Use an online tuner to tune your instrument.
18. Play on!

CHAPTER FIVE
Laser and Vinyl Cutter Projects

Laser cutters cut patterns and shapes into wood, felt, and plastic. The speed and strength of the laser can be increased or decreased, which determines the depth of a cut for a particular substance. Some 2D parts can be punched out and snapped together (or press-fit) into 3D objects. A vinyl cutter is similar to a printer but uses a cutting blade instead of a printing head and cuts thin

Vinyl cutters used can be used to make heat transfer designs, vehicle signs, and banners of varying sizes. The sharp blades allow for very precise cuts.

sheets of vinyl or cardboard instead of paper. These cutters can make letters, shapes, and signs.

PROJECT 4: PLAN A MUSEUM EXHIBITION

This is a two-part project. This chapter will help you set up your own exhibition space for a self-curated museum. For part one of this project, we'll be using a vinyl cutter to make some professional-looking signs for the exhibit. The second part of this project involves 3D printing your own items. When you've completed this project, turn to chapter 8 for more instructions, or remix the project using your own style and ideas.

SKILL LEVEL

Easy to medium

TIME

2 hours

BASIC MATERIALS

Graph paper	Small lamp
Laptop or computer monitor	Extension cords and power strips
Table and tablecloth	Card stock
Pens and markers	Corkboard
Office supplies (stapler, glue, tape, scissors, and so on)	Recycled materials

LASER AND VINYL CUTTER PROJECTS

STEPS

1. Plan the exhibit. Your first step is to find a theme. Think about the focus of your display. In the world of social studies, there are many subjects from which to draw.
2. Your next step is to figure out where the exhibition will be. You can choose your garage, library, or local makerspace. Know the size of your space so that everything you plan to display will fit.
3. Plan your layout. Use graph paper or use an online floor planner to decide where things will go.
4. You can make your exhibit interactive with a computer. Think about what you'd like to do with it. You can display your photos, video, or recorded audio to make your display more interesting. Take a look at the audio and video projects in chapter 6. See how they may fit your vision.
5. You're going to need signs and display materials. You can make the signs by hand with the art supplies listed as basic materials if you're feeling artistic. If you'd prefer to print your signs, follow the instructions for project 5. Use the table, tablecloth, lamp, and any other items from the basic materials list to build your exhibition space. Try to reuse or recycle what you or friends may already have for your displays instead of buying something new.

10 GREAT MAKERSPACE PROJECTS USING SOCIAL STUDIES

PROJECT 5: MAKE A LASER-CUT JIGSAW PUZZLE

Why buy a jigsaw puzzle when you can make one? The first step is to pick an image. Choose any one you'd like: Mount Rushmore, the Great Wall of China, or maybe a scene from ancient Greece. Make multiple copies to give to friends and family to show off your skills and your generosity. For your puzzle, use Inkscape, a vector

The first jigsaw puzzles were made in England in the eighteenth century. They were built using wood and cut after pictures or maps were glued onto them.

LASER AND VINYL CUTTER PROJECTS

graphics editor. The cuts made by laser and vinyl cutters are extremely precise.

Vector graphics are instructions based on measuring points on the drawing, not the pixels that make up the picture. This gives much better resolution. You can find free downloadable user-created extensions and patterns on Inkscape's website.

SKILL LEVEL

Medium

TIME

1–3 hours

BASIC MATERIALS

Cardboard or card stock (⅛" thickness)	Spray adhesive
Pen and paper	Spray acrylic sealer
Photograph or printed image	Inkscape
Ruler	Cutting pad
Hobby knife	Laser cutter

After you've collected these materials, you have a couple of options to complete your project. If you don't have access to a laser cutter, you can download a PDF of a jigsaw puzzle template and use it as a guide instead.

HANDMADE PUZZLE STEPS

1. Print a PDF puzzle template on card stock or another type of paper. You can also draw your own puzzle grid on the

10 GREAT MAKERSPACE PROJECTS USING SOCIAL STUDIES

back of your cardboard backing.
2. Load the paper back into the printer. Print your image over the template.
3. Measure your picture and the cardboard for your backing. If they're not the same size, trim the cardboard with the ruler and hobby knife to get the straightest edges possible.
4. Use the spray adhesive to attach your picture to the cardboard backing. Let it dry.
5. Use the spray acrylic sealer to give the puzzle a glossy protective finish.
6. Use the hobby knife to hand-cut your puzzle.

LASER CUT PUZZLE STEPS

1. Open Inkscape.
2. Download a laser-cut jigsaw extension from Inkscape.
3. Open the file and copy it to Edit > Preferences > System > User extensions.
4. Restart Inkscape to make the extension available to use.
5. Load the jigsaw puzzle extension.
6. Import your picture.
7. Click on Dimensions and make sure that the puzzle template and your image are the same size.
8. Choose the number of pieces across and down you want the puzzle to have.
9. Click Apply.
10. Make sure the puzzle outline and picture are aligned using the Align command.
11. Save your file for printing and cutting.

CHAPTER SIX
Audio and Video Projects

In makerspaces, computers can take almost any project to the next level. They can be used to add cool touches to arts and crafts projects, send digital files to a 2D or 3D printer, and create and edit pictures or digital images. If moving beyond traditional craft tools is a goal of yours, creating with a computer or tablet is a great starting point.

PROJECT 6: SING ALONG WITH HISTORY

Like the cigar box guitar, singing was a way for people to express themselves through music with very little cost. The cheapest musical instrument is always your own voice.

Like the computer files that instruct CNC cutters and routers, sheet music gives musicians directions on playing a piece of music.

10 GREAT MAKERSPACE PROJECTS USING SOCIAL STUDIES

Music is entertaining, but it also has other purposes. Songs can make you dance, tell stories, or work for social change.

Do some research and find a song that you'd like to sing along with. You can even step off this continent and find music from a faraway culture. For first timers, pick a song that's relatively simple—it will make this process easier. For this recording session, we're going to use Garage Band, which comes installed on Macs. If your makerspace uses PCs, you can use Audacity. It's open-source audio software that you can download for free for Mac and Windows. If your local making facility has a recording setup with a different program, that will also work.

Before you begin, it's a good idea to get familiar with what the software can do. Experiment a little. You should also do the same with the song you choose. Make sure you know the lyrics and when the vocals start and stop. Make your recording as simple or complex as you'd like. You even can open another empty track and play along—maybe with your new cigar box guitar. Your completed song can also become part of your museum exhibition.

SKILL LEVEL

Easy to medium

TIME

1–2 hours

BASIC MATERIALS

Computer (Mac or PC)	Garage Band
USB microphone	Headphones

AUDIO AND VIDEO PROJECTS

Tech Camps

If you'd like to combine learning new things with the fun of summer camp, consider attending a tech camp. These summer programs are a great way to connect with other students who share your interests. Who knows—you may find yourself working on a project with someone in another city or country!

Tech camps cover a wide variety of subjects. Some of these camps are expensive, but many, such as ID Tech (which has camps in more than twenty-five states), offer scholarships to some applicants. Some don't provide full scholarships but may provide financial assistance with room and board or travel expenses. Some are free, but those can be more competitive. You may need to do some research to find one. Start with local libraries, museums, high schools, state colleges, and universities.

Want to create but can't travel? Why not try a virtual summer camp? The folks at Google+ and Maker Media have joined forces to sponsor Maker Camp. Maker Camp is a six-week camp that you can attend online every day. The only money you may have to spend would be for supplies (and snacks). Check out what they offer at **Makercamp.com**.

10 GREAT MAKERSPACE PROJECTS USING SOCIAL STUDIES

STEPS

1. Find a song you'd like to sing along with. If you're having trouble, take a look at some of the public domain music websites listed in the back of this book. Garage Band can work with multiple file formats.
2. Open Garage Band. Connect your USB microphone and headphones.
3. Create an audio project using a microphone or line input. You'll see an empty track called Audio 1. This is where your vocals will be recorded.
4. Import the track you want to add your vocal track to by using the menu or dragging the file into the recording area of the screen.
5. Record your new vocals and any other touches you'd like to add.
6. If you make a mistake, you can select and delete the recording before you begin again.
7. When you're satisfied with your session, save your file.

PROJECT 7: PHOTO EDIT YOURSELF INTO HISTORY

Without a time machine, the best way to send yourself back in time may be to use photo editing software. It's fun and a great way to learn about different time periods. Figure out a time in history that you're interested in, and choose something from then. The possibilities are endless. You could

AUDIO AND VIDEO PROJECTS

Manipulating photos and other digital media is very common in the design stage of making things. Software and online tools have made this easier over the past twenty years.

even use your doctored selfies in your museum exhibition. This project uses a free online photo editor called BeFunky.com. PicMonkey.com is another similar website. If the computer you're using has Adobe Photoshop, you can use that as well. The steps may be different using other photo editors, so you may have to experiment a little or watch an online tutorial for help.

SKILL LEVEL

Easy to medium

TIME

1 hour

BASIC MATERIALS

Photo	BeFunky online photo editor
Computer (Mac or PC) or tablet (iOS, Android, or Windows)	PicMonkey (optional)

STEPS

1. Upload the photo you've chosen to send back in time. You can also digitize a photo or drawing of your own by using a scanner or taking a digital photo.
2. Once your photo is loaded, select Layer Manager (it's the top icon on the left). From the menu, choose Add Layer.
3. A box for Layer Properties will pop up. Choose Cutout.
4. The Cutout box has five options for Shape Selection. Choose one and use it to trace around the part of your photo that you're going to insert.
5. Use the Feather tool to make your cutout image smoother.
6. Click on Export as Layer to save your cutout to the Layer Manager.

AUDIO AND VIDEO PROJECTS

7. Upload your background picture. Experiment with some of the other editing tools to see what they can do to your photo.
8. Click on the Layer Manager again. Drag your cutout onto your background picture.
9. Resize the cutout if needed. When you've got your placement set, click on Flatten Layers. This will merge your background photo and your cutout.
10. Save your new blended photo.

CHAPTER SEVEN
3D-Printing Projects

PROJECT 8: DESIGN AND MAKE YOUR OWN BOARD GAME

This project combines both digital fabrication and arts and crafts. First, you'll make your game board using simple materials. The rules are wide open. You can model your game after checkers or chess and substitute 3D pieces, or you can invent a brand-new game with brand-new rules.

Chess was first played in the sixth century. Before it reached the New World, it was enjoyed by players in India, China, and Persia.

3D-PRINTING PROJECTS

Think Big, Print Big

We know some of the amazing things that can be accomplished with 3D printing today, but the future may hold much more than we can imagine. Most 3D printers in makerspaces are of the desktop variety, so what they can fabricate is limited by size. However, larger objects can be built by printing and connecting smaller pieces.

(continued on the next page)

3D printers are used to make both small and large objects. Completion time depends on the size of the printed item.

10 GREAT MAKERSPACE PROJECTS USING SOCIAL STUDIES

(continued from the previous page)

But what are some of the biggest single things that can be made with a 3D printer? It all depends on the size of the printer. One of the largest on Earth is China's Winsun 3D Printer. It's 132 feet (40 meters) long, 33 feet (10 meters) wide, and 22 feet (7 meters) tall. In other words, it's huge. The Winsun printer can print houses and even a five-story building. It also uses recycled content to make these large structures, which saves money and has less impact on the environment.

Next, make your game pieces using Cura. It's 3D slicing software that tells a 3D printer how to make an object. This software does what the name suggests—it takes a 3D model and slices or splits it up into small two-dimensional pieces to print an object bit by bit. It has two modes: Basic for people who are new to using the software and Expert for those who have some experience and want to step up their designs. Once the instructions are sent, the 3D printer does the rest of the work.

It's important to get some experience using the software. Before you move to the printing phase of this project, be sure to try your hand at importing STL (STereoLithography) files and seeing what you can do with them. STL is a file format read by most computer-aided design (CAD) software.

SKILL LEVEL

Easy to medium

TIME

3–4 hours

BASIC MATERIALS

20" x 20" and 1/16" thick piece of cardboard or plastic	Duct tape
Ruler	Permanent markers
Scissors	Spray acrylic sealer
Pencil	3D printer
Hobby knife	SD card

GAME BOARD STEPS

1. The average game board is 18" x 18". Use your ruler or straight edge to measure that area and trim off the extra material.
2. Use the ruler to measure 9". Mark the spot and draw a line that evenly divides the board.
3. Use the hobby knife and ruler to cut the board in half.
4. Evenly line up the two pieces. Use duct tape to connect the two halves on both sides.
5. Use duct tape on all of the board edges to make it sturdier.
6. Design your board. Hand draw the playing surface or use drawing software and a printer.

10 GREAT MAKERSPACE PROJECTS USING SOCIAL STUDIES

7. Use spray acrylic sealer to protect your board.

GAME PIECES STEPS

1. Open Cura and select the 3D printer you're using when prompted. Stay in Basic mode.
2. Load and open your 3D model. If you don't have one, look on 3D depositories like Thingiverse, MakerShop, or MyMiniFactory.
3. When your model is loaded, explore what the software can do. Choose Layer View to see what the spliced version, not your object, looks like.
4. Use Solid View to examine the 3D model using the Mirror, Rotate, and Scale buttons.
5. Click on Enable Support in case your object has hanging pieces.
6. Be sure to select Uniform Scaling if you blow up or shrink your 3D model.
7. Adjust the print quality. See how long it takes for low and high quality. Make your choice depending on how much time you'd like to spend printing. Remember, you're going to be printing quite a few pieces. Use the lowest quality if you're trying to see a rough model of your object.
8. Convert your file into GCode. This is the instruction language that the 3D printer will understand. You can select it when you click the Save to Disk button.
9. Copy your GCode file onto an SD card.
10. Insert the SD card in a 3D printer and wait for your game pieces or tokens.

PROJECT 9: 3D PRINT YOUR MUSEUM EXHIBITS

SKILL LEVEL

Easy to medium

TIME

3–8 hours

Let's finish the museum project we started back in chapter 5. What's a museum exhibit without anything to display? Follow the same steps from project 4. Do some research and pick models according to your theme. For example, the Smithsonian Museum has an online repository of free 3D files to print. Many important objects from the nineteen museums that make up the Smithsonian Institution are available, as are artifacts and models from the US Space Program and many of its missions to outer space.

PROJECT 10: CREATE YOUR OWN PROJECT

By now, you should have a good idea of what you're capable of making. Your final assignment? Create your own assignment! This is a huge part of the maker spirit. The projects in this

10 GREAT MAKERSPACE PROJECTS USING SOCIAL STUDIES

book are just an introduction to some of the things you can make and create.

There's only one rule that you *absolutely must* follow: nothing is a mistake! Simple, right? If you've tried some of these projects but don't feel confident, don't worry. Create a project that you feel you can do, and build on those skills. Remember, the maker community is all about sharing and collaboration. Ask other makers or mentors at your local makerspace for help. There are no deadlines or due dates in the book. Take your time. What if you fail the first time? You're never really failing because you're always learning. Practice makes perfect.

On the other hand, if you feel that these projects aren't challenging enough, great! Design something with which you may have difficulty. Try your hand at something more complicated like electronics, robotics, or computers. If you're planning something bigger, be sure to plan and see what skills and tools you'll need.

Makerspaces are hotbeds of creativity. You can learn a skill, make friends, and learn to work in teams. These are all skills that are going to be necessary in the future. The world is getting smaller thanks to the internet and social media, and countries around the world are more connected than ever before. Problems that used to affect only part of our planet now have the potential to involve all of us. Some of these problems are so large that it will take a combined effort from people around the globe. Social studies is a great starting point for understanding these issues.

GLOSSARY

artifact An object from the past that was used by ancient people.
CAD An abbreviation for computer-aided design software that can be used to create or modify 3D computer models.
civics The study of people and how they behave in a society.
collaboration Working together.
DIY (Do-It-Yourself) Creating or making things on your own.
exhibition A display or showing of a collection of items such as artwork or artifacts.
Fab Lab An abbreviation for Fabrication Laboratory, a facility where people can use a common set of tools and equipment to make and create things.
fabricate To make an object or thing.
funding Money raised for a project or facility.
hack To alter or make changes to an existing program, object, or technology.
hackathon A collaborative coding or programming session that can last from a few hours to a few days.
hackerspace Another name for a makerspace.
industrial Happening in a factory or place for manufacturing.
mentor A person who helps and gives advice.
open source Software, hardware, or code that users can use or change for free.
pixel The smallest part of a picture or image.
repository A digital archive of downloadable 3D-object files.
social sciences The study of people and how they interact with each other.
STEAM An acronym for science, technology, engineering, art, and math.
3D model A mathematical or computer model of a real object.

Design Fabrication Zone (DFZ)
Ryerson University
285 Victoria Street
Toronto, ON M5B 2K3
Canada
(416) 979-5188
Website: http://dfz.ryerson.ca
The DFZ is a hub for "design/fabrication innovation and entrepreneurship" at Ryerson University. They also offer free training in 3D scanning and printing at their "3DFZ Workshops."

échoFab
355 Peel St, Suite 111
Montreal, Quebec, H3C2G9
Canada
(514) 855-4500
Website: https://www.fablabs.io/labs/echofab
échoFab is the first MIT-accredited Fab Lab in Canada. It offers workshops and holds events.

Fab Foundation
50 Milk Street, 16th Floor
Boston, MA 02109
(857) 333-7777
Website: http://www.fabfoundation.org
The Fab Foundation is dedicated to both "bringing digital fabrication tools and process to people of all ages."

FOR MORE INFORMATION

The Franklin Institute
222 North 20th Street
Philadelphia, PA 19103
(215) 448-1200
Website: https://www.fi.edu
The Franklin Institute is a science museum and educational research facility that offers interactive exhibits and monthly challenges for makers.

Maker Faire
c/o Maker Media
1160 Battery Street, #125
San Francisco, CA 94111
(877) 306-6253
Website: http://makerfaire.com
In the words of Maker Media, Maker Faire is the "Greatest Show (& Tell) on Earth." Maker Faires are held all around the world each year, giving aspiring and veteran makers the opportunity to network and create.

WEBSITES

Because of the changing nature of internet links, Rosen Publishing has developed an online list of websites related to the subject of this book. This site is updated regularly. Please use this link to access this list:

http://www.rosenlinks.com/UMFSP/socialstudies

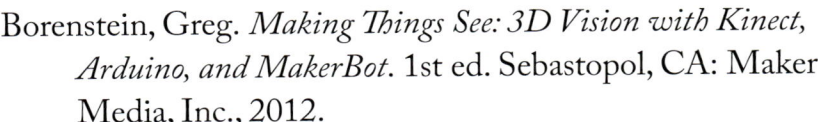

FOR FURTHER READING

Borenstein, Greg. *Making Things See: 3D Vision with Kinect, Arduino, and MakerBot*. 1st ed. Sebastopol, CA: Maker Media, Inc., 2012.

Busmen, Isaac, and Anthony Rotolo. *The Book on 3D Printing*. Scotts Valley, CA: CreateSpace Independent Publishing Platform, 2013.

Cameron, Schrylet, and Carolyn Craig. *STEM Labs for Middle Grades, Grade 5–8*. Greensboro, NC: Mark Twain Media, 2016.

Cline, Lydia. *3D Printing with Autodesk 123D, TinkerCAD, and MakerBot*. Columbus, OH: McGraw-Hill Education TAB, 2014.

Editors of MAKE. *Make: The Ultimate Guide to 3D Printing*. 1st ed. Sebastopol, CA: Maker Media, Inc., 2012.

Frenkel, Andrew. *50 STEM Labs—Science Experiments for Kids*. Vol. 1. Scotts Valley, CA: CreateSpace Independent Publishing Platform, 2014.

Haber, Louis. *Black Pioneers of Science and Invention*. Boston, MA: HMH Books for Young Readers, 1992.

Kelly, James Floyd. *3D Modeling and Printing with Tinkercad: Create and Print Your Own 3D Models*. Indianapolis, IN: Que Publishing, 2014.

Murphy, Maggie. *High-Tech DIY Projects with 3D Printing*. New York, NY: PowerKids Press, 2014.

Norris, Donald. *The Internet of Things: Do-It-Yourself at Home Projects for Arduino, Raspberry Pi, and Beaglebone Black*. 1st ed. Columbus, OH: McGraw-Hill Education TAB, 2015.

Roza, Greg. *Getting the Most Out of Makerspaces to Make Musical Instruments*. New York, NY: Rosen Classroom, 2014.

BIBLIOGRAPHY

All3DP. "26 Biggest 3D Printers in the World (Right Now)." *Features*. July 13, 2016. https://all3dp.com/biggest-3d-printers-world.

"Benjamin Franklin." Retrieved October 13, 2016. http://www.biography.com/people/benjamin-franklin-9301234.

Davis, Michelle. "A Brief History of Makerspaces." Retrieved January 3, 2017. https://curiositycommons.wordpress.com/a-brief-history-of-makerspaces.

Editors of MAKE. *Make: The Ultimate Guide to 3D Printing*. 1st ed. Sebastopol, CA: Maker Media, Inc., 2012.

Maker Education Initiative. *High School Makerspace Tools and Materials*. Sebastopol, CA: Maker Media, Inc., 2012.

Maker Education Initiative. *Youth Makerspace Playbook*. Sebastopol, CA: Maker Media, Inc., 2013.

McCue, T. J. "First Public Library to Create a Maker Space." *Forbes*, November 15, 2011. http://www.forbes.com/sites/tjmccue/2011/11/15/first-public-library-to-create-a-maker-space/#7845591380da.

Pretty, Leslie B. *School Library Makerspaces: Grades 6–12*. Santa Barbara, CA: Libraries Unlimited, 2012.

Torrone, Phillip. "Is It Time to Rebuild & Retool Public Libraries and Make 'TechShops'?" *Make:*, March 10, 2011. http://makezine.com/2011/03/10/is-it-time-to-rebuild-retool-public-libraries-and-make-techshops.

INDEX

A
Adobe Photoshop, 47
anthropology, 8
Arduino, 21
art, 22, 32, 39
artifact, 22, 55
Audacity, 44

B
biology, 25
board game design, 50–54
buoyancy, 30

C
cigar box guitar, 31–36
civics, 9
climate, 8, 9
computer-aided design (CAD), 17, 18, 22, 24, 52
computers, 5, 14, 16–18, 21, 23, 24, 29, 38, 39, 44, 47, 48, 52, 56
Cura, 52

D
design, 11, 16, 18, 19, 24–25, 37, 47, 50–53, 56

E
economics, 8, 9
Edison, Thomas, 12
Egypt, 25–26, 39
Egyptian papyrus project, 25–28

F
Fab Labs, 14, 17
Franklin, Benjamin, 10–11

G
Garage Band, 44–45
geography, 7, 8, 9, 22
Gershenfeld, Neil, 15

H
hackerspace, 14
history, 8, 22

I
Inkscape, 40–42

J
jigsaw puzzle, 40–42

L
laser cutters, 18, 19, 37, 41
law, 8, 25
Lego, 21
libraries, 23–24, 39

M
Macs, 44, 48
Make: magazine, 16
Maker Faires, 16
makerspace,
   beginnings, 15–16
   definition of, 14
   safety in, 19–20

INDEX

today, 16–17
tools used in, 17–21
Massachusetts Institute of Technology (MIT), 15
math, 24
mentor, 14, 56
museum exhibition project, 38–39, 55

N

National Council for the Social Studies, 7

O

office supplies, 20
open source, 21, 44

P

paddleboat project, 29–31
paper, 25–28
PCs, 44, 48
photo editing, 46–49
political science, 8

R

Raspberry Pi, 21
robotics, 21

S

sing along project, 43–46
social media, 9, 11, 46
social sciences, 9
social studies,
  definition, 7
  inventing and, 12–13
  subjects, 8
sociology, 8
STEAM, 22,
STL files, 52

T

tech camps, 45
3D printers, 18–19, 37, 43, 51–54
3D scanners, 18

V

vinyl cutters, 19, 37, 38, 41

10 GREAT MAKERSPACE PROJECTS USING SOCIAL STUDIES

ABOUT THE AUTHOR

Kerry Hinton has been fascinated with the world of making since he was in grade school. When he read the first issue of *Make:* in 2005, he decided to dive even deeper into making. He was a member of both the stage crew and the audio-visual squad in high school and loved getting involved in collaborative projects. Since then, he's written books on hackathons and 3D scanning to help kids of all ages embrace STEAM and the art of making in the twenty-first century. He lives in Hoboken, New Jersey, and is planning to attend the next World Maker Faire in New York City.

PHOTO CREDITS

Cover, pp. 1, 15 Christian Science Monitor/Getty Images; pp. 4–5 Rawpixel.com/Shutterstock.com; pp. 7, 14, 22, 29, 37, 43, 50 (background) MuchMania/Shutterstock.com; p. 8 ibreakstock/Shutterstock.com; p. 10 Stocksnapper/Shutterstock.com; p. 12 Kichigin/Shutterstock.com; p. 18 Grigvovan/Shutterstock.com; p. 23 Jetta Productions/Digital Vision/Thinkstock; p. 26 francesco de marco/Shutterstock.com; p. 32 Lawrence K. Ho/Los Angeles Times/Getty Images; p. 34 attem/Shutterstock.com; p. 37 jurra8/Shutterstock.com; p. 40 VikaSuh/Shutterstock.com; p. 43 Leenvdb/Shutterstock.com; p. 47 © iStockphoto.com/Jaap2; p. 50 Michelangelus/Shutterstock.com; p. 51 Alexander Tolstykh/Shutterstock.com; cover and interior page design elements © iStockphoto.com/Samarskaya (cover wires), © iStockphoto.com/klenger (interior wires), © iStockphoto.com/Steven van Soldt (metal plate), © iStockphoto.com/Storman (background pp. 4–5).

Editor/Photo Researcher: Xina M. Uhl